In the FOOTSTEPS of FRANKLIN

ROGER SMITH

Second Edition

An electronic edition of this book was published in 2000 by eMatter.com.

In the Footsteps of Franklin.

Copyright 1994, 2000, 2008 by Roger Smith. All rights reserved. No part of this book may be reproduced or transmitted in any form or by any means, electronic or mechanical, including photocopying, recording, or by any information storage and retrieval system, without written permission from the author. For information address Modelbenders Press, P.O. Box 781692, Orlando, Florida 32878.

Modelbenders Press books may be purchased for business and promotional use or for special sales. For information please contact the publisher.

PRINTED IN THE UNITED STATES OF AMERICA

Visit our web site at www.modelbenders.com

Designed by Adina Cucicov at Flamingo Designs

The Library of Congress has cataloged the paperback edition as follows:
Smith, Roger
    In the Footsteps of Franklin /
    Roger Smith—2nd ed.
    1. History 2. Business I. Title

ISBN-13: 978-0-9823040-0-6
ISBN-10: 0-9823040-0-5

Table of Contents

Introduction 3
Chapter 1: Industry 5
Chapter 2: Frugality 9
Chapter 3: Friendship 13
Chapter 4: Learning 17
Chapter 5: Reading 23
Chapter 6: Writing 29
Chapter 7: Independence 35
Chapter 8: Agreeable 39
Chapter 9: Humility 45
Chapter 10: Character 49
Chapter 11: Honesty 53
Chapter 12: Enterprising 57
Chapter 13: Optimistic 63
Chapter 14: Travel 67
Chapter 15: Charity 71
Chapter 16: Lucky 77
Chapter 17: Healthy 81
Chapter 18: Habitudes 83
Chapter 19: Thumbnail 87

INTRODUCTION

BENJAMIN FRANKLIN was one of 17 children born to a Boston candle maker. As part of this family he received only two years of formal schooling, but through diligence and good habits rose to be one of the most prominent men of his time and one of the greatest in American history. He received six honorary degrees for universities and was referred to as the "Greatest Philosopher of the Century". Even today we name schools, streets, counties, and children after him.

The Boston Bay in 1854.

During his long life he was successful at many different professions. As a businessman he was a tradesman and a successful printer, establishing several other young men in the profession and benefiting from the relationship. Franklin retired from business as a wealthy man at the age of 42.

He then went on to serve as a local councilman and justice of the peace. He was responsible for leading the establishment of a local police force, fire company, militia, college (now the University of Philadelphia), and hospital. His leisure time was also spent as an inventor, most famous for experiments with electricity, the Franklin stove, and bifocal spectacles.

Franklin was a prolific writer, earning much of his reputation from this. To this day *The Autobiography of Benjamin Franklin*, excerpts from *Poor Richard's Almanac*, *The Way to Wealthy*, *On Writing Well*, and numerous others are sold in bookstores and read widely. He was also the Postmaster General, Ambassador to France, and a member of the constitutional Convention.

The traits that made this man great should be of interest to others seeking to better their position in life. Luckily Franklin himself set down these traits in his autobiography and other writings. He realized that he was a famous figure and strove to pass on to others the habits of his life that were responsible for this success. These habits have been organized an illustrated in the chapters of this book.

INDUSTRY

"IN ORDER TO secure my Credit and Character as a Tradesman, I took care not only to be in Reality Industrious & frugal, but to avoid all Appearances of the Contrary. I dresses plainly; I was seen at no Places of idle Diversion; I never went out a-fishing or Shooting; a Book, indeed, sometimes debauch'd me from my Work; but that was seldom, snug, & gave no Scandal: and to show that I was not above my business. I sometimes brought home the Paper I purchas'd at the stores, thro' the streets on a wheelbarrow. Thus being esteem'd an industrious thriving young Man, and paying duly for what I bought, the Merchants who imported Stationery solicited my Custom, others propos'd supplying me with Books, & I went on swimmingly."

Thus we see how Benjamin Franklin attended his business and became such a success. He also writes of his life with such

Franklin at work on a printing press, by Charles Mills.

CHAPTER
1

color and plainness that it is magnetic reading. *The Autobiography of Benjamin Franklin* would be enjoyable and interesting even if there were no great lessons to be learned from its pages, but the addition of these lessons makes it an even greater treasure.

Franklin plainly states that there are two keys to financial success—Industry and Frugality. These he hails as indispensable and shows his character in them throughout the book.

> "And in my Industry in my Business continu'd as indefatigable as it was necessary. I was in debt for my Printinghouse, I had a young Family coming on to be educated, and I had to contend with for Business two Printers who were established in the Place before me. My circumstances however grew daily easier; my original Habits of Frugality Continuing. And my Father having among his Instructions to me when a Boy, frequently repeated a Proverb of Solomon, "seest thou a Man diligent in his calling, he shall stand before Kings, he shall not stand before mean Men". I from thence consider'd Industry as a means of obtaining Wealth and Distinction".

The solution to competition, to debt, to financial planning—is intelligent, hard work. Without work all intelligence is but the crackling of synapses which feeds no one. Combined with work one man can support many others and further sponsor even more, as Franklin did. Today men carry briefcases presumably containing work. With Franklin's wheelbarrow it was obvious and you didn't see just everyone leaving their shop for the night with a cart full of business in front of them. Did the blacksmith take iron and coals home with him for the evening? Or did the haberdasher carry his hats and frames? Certainly not. When men saw Benjamin Franklin in the street with his printing supplies they took notice and made comment. He was the talk of the town, the gossip in the coffeehouse, and the rumor along the wharf. But, in this he was an active man being discussed by idle men. Other active men took this trait as admirable, not strange, and his public character benefited much from it.

Chapter I: Industry

"... that mention being made of the new Printing Office at the Merchants every-night-Club, the general Opinion was that it must fail, there being already two Printers in the Place, Keimer & Bradford; but Doctor Baird... gave a contrary Opinion; 'for the Industry of that Franklin', says he, 'is superior to any thing I ever saw of the kind: I see him still at work when I go home from Club; and he is at Work again before his Neighbors are out of bed'..."

That Doctors, some of the most respected citizens, took good notice of him speaks well of labor's effect on reputation. This increasing reputation and good Credit with his suppliers led to more business and easier living.

This is his position before the age of thirty and he is just beginning. In fact the prophets of doom were right in a sense - three printers were too many. Keimer's business failed and Bradford's suffered stagnation while Franklin grew daily more successful. And what is the secret of this success? Franklin himself answers—"Industry and Frugality".

As a young man in London he not only worked but worked at the most reputable printing houses where his skills could be tested and enhanced. He labored diligently at Palmer's doing both press work and composing. From there he moved up to Watt's further adding to his skills. These both gave him opportunity to see long established and well equipped printers. This knowledge later stands him in good stead upon his return to American printing houses where he is able to put his unique experience to work in creating new print type, a skill not yet available in the New World.

Though he is devoted to his employer's industry he is also devoted to promoting his own position. A man's work should result in his own success and that of the business. If both are not accomplished, one is using the other. The success of Franklin, an individual, is more than just the prosperity of one man because it is individuals who use their prosperity to promote the welfare of their country, state, city, and fellow citizens. In this case the success of Franklin resulted in the education and furtherance of the printing trade in America. Only when an individual is promoted by his work can that promotion spread to other men. If a man is used rather than improved by an institution, then the growth of the institution will only lead to the usury of more men. The purpose of industry must, therefore, be to promote both the business and the individual.

The value of industry and frugality go far beyond procuring success. "...Industry and Frugality, as a means of procuring Wealth and thereby securing Virtue, it being more-difficult for a Man in Want to act always honestly, as (to use here one of those Proverbs) it is hard for an empty Sack to stand upright." This excellent point is often missed. But how often are we robbed, assaulted, or cheated by men who have risen to wealth through their own hard work? A man who labors for his estate has no need of dishonest means of support. He has confidence in his own abilities to sustain himself and his family. We may, therefore, expect a prosperous and honest man to be built out of industry. Certainly, there are other means of procuring wealth, but do they also build moral character? Do they plant good seeds in the community from which will spring other good men?

"I mention this Industry the more particularly and the more freely, tho' it seems to be talking in my own Praise, that those of my Posterity who shall read it, may know the Use of that Virtue, when they see its Effects in my Favor throughout this Relation."

INDUSTRY:

Be ashamed to catch yourself idle.

FRUGALITY

IT IS CLEAR from Franklin's writing that next to Industry he values Frugality. Indeed, though industry may increase one's income it requires a partner to increase one's wealth. Without Frugality the fruits of Industry are but travelers passing through our hands on the way to a more frugal man. Franklin's goals do not seem to have been to live high and extravagant but rather to increase his standing in the community.

"... propos'd to my Brother, that if he would give me weekly half the Money he paid for my Board I would board myself. He instantly agreed to it, and I presently found that I could save half what he paid me. This was an additional fund for buying Books." He also mentions saving money by eating simple food, avoiding beer, and living without fine possessions. This and other passages show that Benjamin Franklin was

Statue of Ben Franklin in Old City Philadelphia.

CHAPTER
2

not interested in using his money for rich living. The money obtained from Industry is often invested in books and in paying the debt of his friends. He admits a weakness for books and indulges it often, but these serve him well and should be viewed as an investment in future affluence rather than as extravagance. Though he does not explain, he often uses his money to pay the bills of his friends, a weakness which he repeats several times, and each time receives no repayment.

The modern legends of rich men living plainly could have started with Franklin. "... I took care not only to be in Reality Industrious & frugal, but to avoid all Appearances of the Contrary. I dressed plainly; I was seen at no places of idle Diversion...". In communities where men know each other socially it is not fit that one should flaunt his wealth. Others will resent it, especially in hard times, and they will not contribute to the growth of his business. In fact, money is earned through reputation as much as through hard work. Rich food, fine clothes, and frivolous spending will negate the progress you make by industry. It is wise, and expected, that a man behave and talk less well to do than he really is. Since there will then be no boastful proclamations to live up to, he need not spend money to become in reality the man he has made himself in words. The less his reputation for richness grows, the more grows his bank balance.

"We kept no idle servants, our Table was plain and simple, our furniture of the cheapest. For instance my Breakfast was a long time Bread & Milk, (no Tea) and I ate it out of a two penny earthen porriager with a Pewter Spoon." Note the meal of domestic bread and milk, cheaply obtained, and the specific absence of imported and taxed tea. This man controls the draining of his income with the same diligence that he husbands the filling of it. There are two openings in every man's wealth. The first is income which may be increased by Industry. The second is outgo which can be decreased by Frugality. Exercising both practices maximizes the growth of wealth.

In forgoing pleasure he is rather postponing it. He wanted to hold off, let it gather interest in order to enjoyed more fully in the future. His industry and Frugality were vehicles to carry him to wealth and position. He was a commoner making his way to the head of a new nation. Rather than Scrooge he should be compared to an Olympic athlete who forgoes pleasure in order to reach higher goals. And upon obtaining these goals finds that he has access to a richer life than he ever would have otherwise.

Though hard work will be smiled upon by most men, there are far fewer who smile upon frugality. Being frugal is just as hard as being industrious. You will, in all forms, be encouraged to spend what you have earned. Indeed many men have just the strength to earn their money but lack the strength to save it. They are exhausted and allow their hard earned dollars to again slip through their fingers into other waiting hands. If you exercise that extra strength, there will be more dollars resting in your hands and fewer falling to those around you. Only your own conscience will counsel thrift, a voice that is small in comparison to those about you.

> "He drank on however, & had 4 or 5 shillings to pay out of his Wages every Saturday Night for that muddling Liquor; an Expense I was free from. And thus these poor devils keep themselves always under."

FRUGALITY:
Buy what thou hast no need of, and ere long thou shalt sell thy necessaries.

FRIENDSHIP

BENJAMIN FRANKLIN recommends Industry and Frugality for obtaining wealth but throughout his autobiography he exhibits a characteristic which is at least as important to his success as these. No less than thirty times does he recall friendships and acquaintances with other people. In fact his general attitude toward others is one of respect and affection. Today it seems unusual to characterize a successful man as friendly, but this is the most glaring characteristic of Franklin throughout his life.

Of Dr. Brown, "He entered into Conversation with me while I took some Refreshment, and finding I had read a little, became very sociable and friendly. Our Acquaintance continu'd as long as he lived." Again, "But the Governor inquir'd for me, came up, & with a Condescension & Politeness I had been quite unus'd too, made me many Compliments,

Benjamin Franklin is credited with the creation of the first pair of bifocals in the early 1760s.

CHAPTER
3

desired to be acquainted with me, blam'd me kindly for not having made myself known to him when I first came to the Place, and would have me away with him to the Tavern."

Throughout life his attitude toward others is one of warmth and devotion. Often he refers to men as his friends until their death. Whether he meant to or not these friendships also brought him much opportunity and business. They seem to have had as big a part in his success as did Industry and Frugality, if not bigger.

"I soon obtain'd, thro' my Friend Hamilton, the Printing of the New Castle Paper Money, another profitable Job."

"...every one of these exerting themselves in recommending Business to us. Breintnal particularly procur'd us from the Quakers, the Printing 40 Sheets of their History...".

"I who was intimately acquainted with him, (being employ'd in printing his Sermons and Journals, & c.)".

The source of much of his business was friends. These he seems always to be acquiring. He finds them in governors, colonels, committee men, doctors, ministers, printers, hired hands, land-ladies, recluses, and fellow travelers. He genuinely loved people and it shows throughout the account of his life. These people bore him good will, bringing in business, providing favorable conditions for rent, advising him of future trouble, warning him away from those of bad character, and giving him nothing in return. He was not a glad-hander for profit, but a genuinely warm person.

This characteristic is indispensable to a man who needs the support of others in his business and life, a condition which defines all men. The reclusive, unsociable man will never experience the level of success and happiness known by those who touch others with their life. Men's lives are not islands, cut off from contact with others by an ocean of worldly cares. Rather each is like one mountain in an entire range. It is connected to those about it and through them to every other mountain.

Chapter 3: Friendship

Small business men meet every morning at the local cafe for coffee. They do not intend a purpose for each day but rather share the burden and feel the comraderie of the town. Each establishes relationships which result in a network of business exchange. The man who is too busy or not of the temperament for these meetings will miss the success he could have otherwise enjoyed.

The picture of a bespectacled man surrounded with books misleads us into believing that Franklin had no personality for people. This was absolutely not the case. In fact, books and their learning were often the basis of his strongest friendships. They lead to acquaintances with the most influential men of the community. One set of these literary friends formed the first library for public use in the New World.

While working at a new printing job Franklin records, "At Burlington I made an Acquaintance with many principal people of the Province. Several of them had been appointed by the Assembly a Committee to attend the Press, and take Care that no more Bills were printed than the Law directed. They were therefore by Turns constantly with us, and generally he who attended brought with him a Friend or two for Company. My Mind having been much more improv'd by Reading than Keimer's, I suppose it was for that Reason my Conversation seem'd to be more valu'd. They had me to their Houses, introduc'd me to their Friends and show'd me much Civility, while he (Keimer), tho' the Master, was a little neglected." These men included a judge, the secretary of the province, members of the assembly, and the Surveyor General. As he lived he continued to collect friendships with such men and continues to gain business from them. And not just business, but his position in the community increased until he was himself one of the influential men that he once befriended.

Isaac Decon, the Surveyor General, who **"had now by his Industry acquir'd a good estate"** professed of Franklin, **"I forsee, that you will soon work this Man (Keimer) out of his Business & make a fortune in it at Philadelphia."** This is exactly what he did. Franklin's work when he opened his own shop was so superior and his relationships so far reaching that he took much business away from Keimer. This competitor was obliged to sell his business to David Harry and retire to Barbados. And David Harry in turn had the same fate.

But, did he befriend men only as a business opportunity? Of his land-lady, "She was lame in her knees with the Gout, and therefore seldom stirr'd out of her Room, so sometimes wanted company; and hers was so highly amusing to me; that I was sure to spend an Evening with her whenever she desir'd it." Of a 70 year old fellow tenant, "I was permitted once to visit her: She was cheerful & polite, & convers'd pleasantly." No, he was definitely a man affectionate toward others. It was no business strategy but a deep part of his character.

FRIENDSHIP:

We must all hang together, else we shall all hang separately.

LEARNING

ONE OF FRANKLIN'S important habits was to learn. He applied his mind to acquiring skills and knowledge from the first of his life and continued at it until the last. Not just the learning from books, which is so dominant today, but also the learning of skills from people.

"I was put to the Grammar School at Eight Years of age, my Father intending to devote me as the Tithe of his Sons to the Service of the Church. My early Readiness in learning to read (which must have been very early, as I do not remember when I could not read) and the Opinion of all his Friends that I should certainly make a good scholar, encourag'd him in this Purpose of his." Obviously Franklin's family recognized the agility of his mind. He showed it toward books and toward all of life. Many subjects drew his interest and he endeavored to master them. Though he

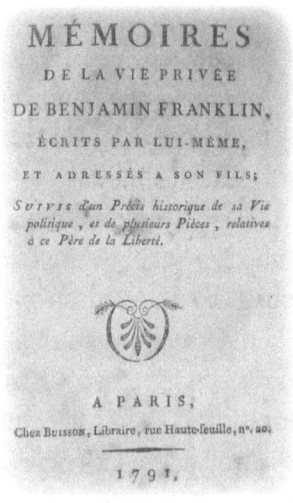

Title page of the very first edition of the autobiography of Benjamin Franklin. The work was originally published in French in 1791 by Buisson, Paris.

CHAPTER 4

did not remain long "Tithed to the Church", he certainly did turnout to be a "good scholar".

"... living near the Water, I was much in and about it, learned early to swim well, & to manage Boats, and when in a Boat or Canoe with other Boys I was commonly allow'd to govern, especially in any case of Difficulty; and upon other Occasions I was generally a leader among the Boys, and sometimes lead them into Scrapes,".

This was a bit over the age of ten, perhaps as an early teenager.

Though his Father was a Candle Maker, a business not given much to mental growth, he went out of his way to see that the children had an opportunity to exercise their minds.

"At his Table he lik'd to have as often as he could, some sensible Friend or Neighbor, to converse with, and always took care to start some ingenious or useful Topic of Discourse, which might tend to improve the Minds of his Children. By this means he turn'd our Attention to what was good, just, & prudent in the Conduct of Life."

This simple man was wise in showing his children that they had muscles beneath their scalps as well as in their backs. They were devoted to an exercise program designed to develop these and which then set them on a different path than that which manual labor may have laid for them. He may also have been creating an inconvenience for himself, for as his children grew they were not as likely to step into the well worn path of tradition, behaving respectably until their deaths. In fact Benjamin disobeyed his father and left Boston for New York and Pennsylvania to escape the indenture to his elder brother. He also abandoned the family religion and formed for himself his own moral philosophy. This philosophy was much based on what he learned at church but was supplemented with common sense and the teachings of philosophers, such as Socrates. Franklin learned to learn and he learned to think, perhaps while sitting at table in his father's house. Though his mind and body were small at the time, learning taught him that the mind does not solidify at a certain size and remain incapable of growth. Rather, a man can grow in mind for many more years and to a much greater stature than he can grow in body.

Franklin put skills into his hands, or perhaps his father did, to ward off the spirit of the sea which threatened to seize him and carry him away. "He therefore sometimes took me to walk with him, and see Joiners, Bricklayers, Turners, Braziers, & c. at their Work, that he might observe my Inclination, & endeavor to fix it on some trade or other on Land. It has ever since been a Pleasure to me to see good Workmen handle their Tools; and it has been useful to me, having learned so much by it, as to be able to do some little Jobs myself in my House, when a Workman could not readily be got; & to construct little Machines for my Experiments while the Intention of making the Experiment was fresh & warm in my Mind." These skills aided and encouraged him in his work with electricity and the Pennsylvania stove. Without these skills he may not have been as ready to delve into some of the questions posed by the sciences.

He taught himself writing, the principle means of his livelihood and fame, by working at little methods to acquire the skill. Of an issue of the Spectator, "I thought the Writing excellent, & wish'd if possible to imitate it. With that View, I took some of the papers, making short Hints of the Sentiment in each Sentence, laid them by a few Days, and then without looking at the Book tried to complete the Papers again". This was followed by an examination of the original and the correcting of his own version. He then embarked on a project in which he converted the text into poems, put it aside awhile, then taking it up turned the poems back into text. This he also took the trouble to compare and correct. He must have met with some success as he humbly refers to small improvements he made in the originals during these exercises.

Next he tells us of endeavoring to teach himself mathematics which he had twice failed to learn at school. Toward this end he went through two popular books on the subject, mastering it to a degree that he no longer need be ashamed of his ignorance.

Following that he instructs himself in Grammar which lead to and introduction to and fascination with the Socratic method of dispute.

A man so active at acquiring skills and knowledge can not be out of work, nor can he remain an ordinary citizen. Though many of the skills seem to be disconnected he always finds useful application of them. They form a foundation; indeed a pyramid, on which to stand and address the world.

This was just the beginning, in England he learned to make print type and to do engraving. These skills being totally absent in America he was invaluable upon his return. These were the basis for a very hansom job with a Philadelphia printer and, when he had set up his own shop, the means for much business in making the first paper money in the New World. Making engravings for the money threw him into company with many of the fine friends mentioned in the previous chapter. Thus, one characteristic—learning—compliments another—Friendship. These in turn support Industry, giving him the wealth with which to exercise Frugality.

Even Franklin's personal character was teachable. **"But a Quaker Friend having kindly inform'd me that I was generally thought proud; that my Pride show'd itself frequently in Conversation; that I was not content with being in the right when discussing a Point, but was overbearing & rather insolent; of which he convinc'd me by mentioning several Instances;—I determined endeavoring to cure myself if I could of this Vice or Folly."** It is difficult to admit that you can learn skills from men, but to admit that you can learn moral character and requires a man truly dedicated to learning, growing, and becoming more than he was born and bred.

We have only begun to explore Franklin's interest in learning. He refused to spend time playing chess with a friend unless the loser of each game agreed to learn a piece of Italian grammar, and they **"thus beat one another into that language"**. He also taught himself French at this time, around to age of 27. These skills contributed much to his advancement in the direction of becoming the first American Ambassador to France.

Franklin had a very active and broad curiosity which led to learning in many areas. He observed the time it took to fell a tree, the behavior of men under lax and strenuous working conditions, the implementation of Indian fire holes, the construction methods and marriage customs of the Quakers, the building and rigging of ships, the effects of vegetable diets, and the practice of writing poetry. All of these he refers to with the greatest of enthusiasm, revealing his active mind and experimental nature. He wanted to conduct a series of experiments concerning the method of building and loading ships and the setting of their sails. Always eager to know the facts behind an event, these experiments were intended to settle the differences of opinion among captains and ship builders who were want to do things their own way and investigate no other.

One of the most fascinating facts was Franklin's experience with electricity. Though few of the details are revealed in the autobiography (but can be found in other works) there is one most important. Franklin is probably best known to all of America for his discovery of certain principles of electricity. But, what is less known is that he was first introduced to the field in 1746 at the age of 40. He had already retired from the printing business, at which he had earned notable wealth, and was being called upon by the community for various public services.

> "...I had secur'd Leisure during the rest of my Life, for Philosophical Studies and Amusements; I purchas'd all Dr. Spence's Apparatus, who had come from England to lecture here; and I proceeded in my Electrical Experiments with great Alacrity..."

Beginning at this late age Benjamin Franklin proceeds to discover and display some of the most useful scientific principles now known to man. At an age when many men have set down upon life and look no further into new business, Franklin was beginning like a young man. A lifetime of learning and curious observation had surely built his mind into a fine explorer of this new world. He illustrated the fact that all learning is valuable, regardless of its practical application, for its gymnastic and strengthening effect upon the mind. From the Autobiography it is doubtful that a single mental muscle went un-exercised inside Benjamin's brain.

It seems most men age their minds much faster than it ages itself. They deprive it of challenging tasks and relegate it to those of rote and drudgery. It turns old, inelastic, brittle, and petrified early and thus atrophies, an embarrassing state for the greatest and most capable tool.

LEARNING:
They that won't be counselled, can't be helped.

READING

FRANKLIN LEARNED to read very young for the 1700's, at least before the age of 10. "From a child I was fond of Reading, and all the little Money that came into my hands was ever laid out in Books. Pleas'd with the Pilgrim's Progress, my first collection was of John Bunyan's Work".

Unfortunately he says "My Father's little Library consisted chiefly of Books on polemic Divinity, most of which I read, and have since often regretted, that at a time when I had such a Thirst for knowedge, more proper Books had not fallen in my Way, since it was now resolved I should not be a Clergyman." When the mind awakens to the outside world it searches for knowledge, for instruction. Then it is important that good, stimulating books be put into a man's hands. These will influence his way of thinking, the morals of life, and the path

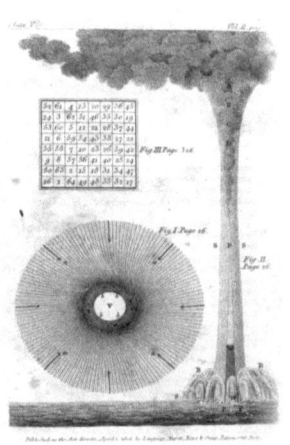

An illustration from Franklin's paper on *"Water-spouts and Whirlwinds."*

CHAPTER
5

he chooses. In any town today there are thousands of books to choose from, most of which are valueless. Our hunger for reading has created an industry that can produce the most sublime and the most urbane writing. This situation is, however, infinitely better than any other. By selecting what you read you are filling your time with entertainment, your mind with learning, and your soul with character. It is possible to satisfy all three of these positively rather than corrupting one for the sake of the other. Men may be your advisors on literature, but they can not be your dictator.

> "Plutarch's Lives there was, in which I read abundantly, and I still think that time spent to great Advantage. There was also a Book of Defoe's called Essays on Projects, and another of Dr. Mather's, called Essays to do Good which perhaps gave me a Turn of Thinking that had an Influence on some of the principal future Events of my Life."

Could these future events have been those of public service: the creation of a Library, Fire company, Police force, and street cleaners. If so, we should attribute these events to ideas planted in Franklin by books. Had he not read these it is possible that a fire company would not have been formed until much later. As a result many more homes may have burned totally to the ground, thereby leaving families destitute. How many men retained their status, how many children had warm homes and thus lived rather than died because Benjamin Franklin read a book called *Essays to do Good*? This is the power of books—not the ivory towered debates often associated with them, but the sharing of ideas and noble characteristics. If those ideas are good we reap good events, if the ideas are bad we reap foul behavior.

It was a book that set Franklin's religious character, and hence formed his behavior in life.

> "Some Books against Deism fell into my Hands; they were said to be the Substance of Sermons preached at Boyle's Lectures. It happened that they wrought an Effect on me quite contrary to what

Chapter 5: Reading

was intended by them: For the Arguments of the Deists which were quoted to be refuted, appeared to me much stronger than the Refutations. In short I soon became a thorough Deist."

"An Acquaintance with the Apprentices of Booksellers, enabled me sometimes to borrow a small one, which I was careful to return soon & clean. Often I sat up in my Room reading the greatest Part of the Night, when the Book was borrow'd in the Evening & to be returned early in the Morning lest it should be miss'd or wanted." Miss'd? Missed by who? Certainly by the Bookseller himself. It appears that through friendships Franklin was able to get books on loan through other apprentices without the knowledge of their masters. These must have been good friendships to merit such favors. And Franklin took care not to abuse these favors, returning the books early so that the secret would not be found out. This passion and absorption happens mostly with the young when they find a book whose ideas so absorb them that they can not stop reading it. As men age they are not so often captured like this. Though this may stem from an adult's previous exposure to most ideas, it is also caused by a growing apart from books which have the depth required to fascinate the adult mind. Many get side-tracked into the popular media and miss out on deep literature that has the power to fascinate. Scholars remain in touch with serious books and thus experience this wonder more often than most. It is wise, therefore, to maintain friendships with those who are intimately involved with books. This gives opportunity for helpful advice in reading, and continues a man's growth in ideas. "And after some time an ingenious Tradesman Mr. Matthew Adams who had a pretty collection of Books, & who frequented our Printing house, took Notice of me, invited me to his Library, & very kindly lent me such Books as I chose to read."

"While I lodg'd in Little Britain I made an Acquaintance with one Wilcox a Bookseller, whose Shop was at the next Door. He had an immense Collection of second-hand books. Circulating Libraries were not then in Use; but we agreed that on certain reasonable

Terms which I have now forgotten, I might take, read & return any of his Books. This I esteem'd a great Advantage, & I made as much use of it as I could."

"While I was intent on improving my Language, I met with an English Grammar ... finishing with a specimen of a dispute in the Socratic Method... I was charm'd with it, adopted it, dropped my abrupt contradiction, and positive Argumentation, and put on the humble Inquirer & Doubter." Thus a book affects a man's whole method of discussing topics with others. Franklin learned from the ancients what he otherwise may have learned by experiment over much time, or not at all. By avoiding this repetition we progress into discovery of new ideas and facts. Through books, knowledge becomes an inheritance of society that always grows and never diminishes. It is a form of intellectual evolution carrying later generations into realms they could never have reached otherwise.

Though Franklin did not remain a Socratic disciple all his life, he was forever affected by what he read

"I continu'd this Method some few years, but gradually left it, retaining only the Habit of expressing myself in Terms of modest Diffidence, never using when I advance anything that may possibly be disputed, the words, Certainly, undoubtedly, or any other that give the Air of Positiveness to an Opinion; but rather say, I conceive, or I apprehend a thing to be so or so... This Habit I believe has been of great Advantage to me."

Reading also led Franklin to many valuable acquaintances. Of Dr. Brown "... finding I had read a little, became very sociable and friendly. Our Acquaintance continu'd as long as he liv'd." Then, "The Governor treated me with great Civility, show'd me his Library, which was a very large one, & we had a good deal of conversations about Books & Authors." The value of these friendships was explored in an earlier chapter, here we see the source of some of them.

Learning and reading valuable books does not just happen, one must aid it. "...this Library afforded me the means of Improvement by

Chapter 5: Reading

constant study, for which I set apart an Hour or two each Day; and thus repair'd in some Degree the Loss of the Learned Education my Father once intended for me." "I early absented myself from the Public Assemblies of the Sect, sunday being my Studying-Day." It takes time to acquire this knowledge and character. But is this the sort of time one associates with school work? No, it is time spent in a beloved activity, the same as some do with gardening and sports. When you read what fascinates your mind the time is a pleasure.

READING:

Often I sat up in my room reading the greatest part of the night, when the book was borrow'd in the evening and to be returned early in the morning.

WRITING

IT WAS THROUGH his writing that Franklin earned much of his fortune and built his reputation. Though technically in the printing business his success there was greatly enhanced by the articles and pamphlets he wrote himself. His autobiography is the only one of the founding fathers' that is still popular today, and this may be due to the very interesting and instructional nature of the text.

Sketch of Tun Tavern in the Revolutionary War.

Franklin taught himself to write as a young man. Some time after the age of twelve but before that of sixteen **"I now took a Fancy to Poetry, and made some little Pieces. My Brother, thinking it might turn to account encourag'd me & put me on composing two occasional Ballads... They were wretched stuff, in the Grubstreet Ballad Style, and when they were printed he sent me about the Town to sell them. The first sold wonder-**

CHAPTER
6

fully, the Event being recent, having made a great Noise. This flatter'd my Vanity. But my Father discourag'd me, by ridiculing my Performances, and telling me Verse-makers were always Beggars; so I escap'd being a Poet, most probably a very bad one."

But he was not discouraged from other writing, for immediately preceding this "... but as **Prose Writing has been of great Use to me in the course of my Life, and was a principal Means of my Advancement. I shall tell you how in such a Situation I acquir'd what little Ability I have in that way.**" This is Franklin's way of saying that it is an important part of his life and he feels it is an important skill to possess. He recognized that without it his fortunes and name would be of much smaller proportions. Through writing one learns to express oneself eloquently and clearly, skills also useful in conversation.

"**... a Question was once some how or other started between Collins & me, of the Propriety of educating the Female Sex in Learning, & their Abilities for study. He was of Opinion that it was improper, & that they were naturally unequal to it. I took the contrary side, perhaps a little for dispute sake.**"

On this subject letters were written back and forth requiring each to put his ideas clearly into words. Benjamin's father found the letters and took the opportunity to point out weaknesses in his son's manner of writing, but he made no comment on the subject. These criticisms Franklin took to heart and endeavored to improve his expression.

"About this time I met with an odd volume of the Spectator. It was the third. I had never before seen any of them. I bought it, read it over and over, and was much delighted with it. I thought the writing excellent, and wish'd if possible to imitate it. With that View, I took some to the Papers, & making short Hints of the Sentiment in each Sentence, laid them by a few Days, and then without looking at the Book, try'd to complete the Papers again, by expressing each hinted Sentiment at length & as fully as it had been express'd before, in any Suitable Words, that should come to hand. Then I compar'd my spectator with the Original, discover'd some of my Faults & corrected them."

With this method Benjamin Franklin began teaching himself to write. The devotion to and study of a single good source is something difficult for us to do today. This type of devotion to a work is now reserved for the study of holy books. Christians studying the Bible or Muslims the Koran are the only ones who return again and again to a work until they know it inside and out. The printed word flows through our life like a flooded river. Every morning there are one or more newspapers on our doorsteps. Each afternoon we receive a new supply of mail demanding to be read. At work we are surrounded by writing on professional and administrative topics. There are monthly magazine subscriptions to "get to." And on every corner retail book stands present a new array of colorful items to be read. With all of this to be absorbed just so we can get on to the next day's supply, how can we possibly focus on a single good work and learn from it? This torrent of words is also often of very poor quality. The writers, having the same constant flow attitude, must finish one article or advertisement so they can give their attention to the next one. It is no wonder that so few men can express themselves clearly in writing, they learn quickly from poor examples and become themselves poor examples for their audiences.

Franklin did not stop with that one exercise. He played back and forth with his issue of the Spectator in several different forms. He turned the articles into Verse—put them aside a while and then turned them back to prose again. He jumbled the ideas, then later tried to restore them to their original order, "this was to teach me Method in the Arrangement of Thoughts." His success in these exercises "... encourag'd me to think I might possibly in time come to be a tolerable English Writer, of which I was extremely ambitious."

By reading you do not learn to write well, rather you learn to write like your authors. And without dissecting them many of their subtle methods will escape your notice. But as we learn we must heed two of

Franklin's observations on the activity. Of the Reverend Mr. Whitefield he says "... I am of Opinion, if he had never written anything he would have left behind him a much more numerous and important Sect." For his "Unguarded Expressions and even erroneous Opinions delivered in Preaching might have been afterwards explain'd, or qualify'd by supposing others that might have accompany'd them; or they might have been deny'd; But 'the written letter remains'". Be careful what you write, it will be permanent, and will be there for all to inspect for errors. Second, he observes, of General Lord Loudon's letters, "... his Lordship's Letters were not ready. And yet whoever waited on him found him always at his Desk, Pen in hand, and concluded he must needs write abundantly... Yes, says I now, but he is like St. George on the signs, always on horseback, and never rides on." This is easy to do when you start to doubt your words, your phrases. But you must leap in and use what you have on hand. You will only find better words only by putting to use those you now have at your disposal.

Knowing how he learned to write, what then did Franklin write. "Everything" is not far from truth. At Palmer's printing house he wrote a metaphysical piece which he printed and distributed. This resulted in his being considered by Mr. Palmer as a young man of some ingenuity, though he disagreed with Franklin's principles. He wrote pieces for Mr. Bradford's newspaper under the pseudonym "The Busy Body". Other topics included morals, the necessity of a paper money, the support of the constabulary, the use of a fire company, the importance of defense and schooling, the use of the Pennsylvania fire place (the Franklin Stove), the support of a hospital, the cleaning of streets, support of the British army, and many political arguments.

The purpose of these writings seems to have been self expression, public improvement, and personal advancement. He was greatly interested in improving the mode of common living in America and even had an eye and pen toward this end. The importance of the topics he expresses thus, "some may think these trifling matters not worth mind-

Chapter 6: Writing

ing or relating. But when they consider, that the Dust blown into the eyes of a Single Person, or into a single shop on a windy Day, is but of small Importance, yet the great Number of the Instances in a populous City, and its frequent Repetitions give it Weight & Consequence; perhaps they will not censure very severely those who bestow some Attention to Affairs of this seemingly low Nature. Human Felicity is produc'd not so much by great Pieces of good Fortune that seldom happen, as by little Advantages that occur every Day." Thus he realized that the personality of an area is formed by all of the small things it offers every day. The addition of a single lane for traffic will improve the disposition of the town more than one of their number winning the million dollar lottery.

All of these practices at writing did much for Franklin. The success of his newspaper was owed to this skill. "This was one of the first good Effects of my having learned a little to scribble. another was, that leading Men, seeing a Newspaper now in the hands of one who could also handle a pen, Thought it convenient to oblige & encourage me." Also, "I wrote and printed an anonymous Pamphlet on it, entitled, 'The Nature & Necessity of a Paper Currency'. It was well received by the common People in general; but the Rich Men dislik'd it; for it increas'd and strengthen'd the Clamor for more Money; and they happening to have no Writers among them that were able to answer it, their Opposition slacken'd, & the Point was carried by a Majority in the House. My Friends there, who conceiv'd I had been of Some Service, Thought fit to reward me, by employing me in printing the Money, a very profitable Job, and a great Help to me. This was another Advantage gain'd by my being able to write."

In addition to this his writing on the many public projects mentioned above were instrumental in seeing the project to fruition.

Franklin's writing seems to have several important characteristics. These are its usefulness, simplicity, and value in entertaining.

"In 1732 I first published my Almanack, under the Name of Richard Saunders; it was continu'd by me about 25 Years, commonly call'd Poor Richard's Almanack. I endeavor'd to make it both entertaining and useful, and it accordingly came to be in such Demand that I reap'd considerable Profit from it, vending annually near Ten Thousand. And observing that it was generally read, scarce any Neighborhood in the Province being without it, I considered it as a proper Vehicle for conveying Instruction among the common Peoples".

And a final quote from Franklin's essay *"The Art of Writing"*, " I have thought in general, that whoever would write so as not to displease good Judges should have particular Regard to these Three Things, viz. That his Performance be *smooth*, *clear*, and *short*: For the contrary Qualities are apt to offend, either the Ear, the Understanding, or the Patience."

WRITING:

Prose Writing has been of great use to me in the course of my life, and was the principal means of my advancement.

INDEPENDENCE

AFTER SEEING several of Franklin's characteristics, especially reading, writing, and learning, we begin to suspect that he does not fit into society as an average man. His abundant acquaintances and friendships show that he was not a shy, closed person, in fact several entries in the Autobiography show him to be very independent and willfull. He was determined that his way was right and he was not afraid to stand by those opinions.

This political cartoon by Franklin urged the colonies to join together during the French and Indian War (Seven Years' War).

He begins by showing his pride in a heritage of protestants during the Reformation. "...they were sometimes in Danger of Trouble on Account of their Zeal against Popery. They had got an English Bible, & to conceal & secure it, it was fastened open with Tapes under & within the Frame of a Joint Stool. When my Great Grandfather read in it to his family, he turned up the Joint Stool upon his knees,

CHAPTER
7

turning over the Leaves then under the Tapes. One of the Children stood at the Door to give Notice if he saw the Apparitor coming, who was an Officer of the Spiritual Court. In that Case the Stool was turn'd down again upon its feet, when the Bible remain'd conceal'd under it as before." This anecdote made Franklin proud and he exhibited much of this spirit throughout his life. His inventions were a refusal to accept the world as it was, but having a determination to improve it applied his mind to the task.

In personal matters his will was not broken by disagreements with his brother and father. They would have kept him leashed short as an apprentice to his brother. He decided to steal away to New York secretly aboard ship. While working under his brother he speaks of his **"Aversion to arbitrary Power that has stuck to me thro' my whole Life"** and admits **"Perhaps I was too saucy & provoking."**

But the biggest example of his free and strong mind is his questioning of the popular religion, and his disobedience to its mandates. He was not a "wild" young man but rather he doubted the statements being handed him. And upon investigating these formed his own set of beliefs based upon the available evidence. **"... my indiscreet Disputations about Religion began to make me pointed at with Horror by good People, as an Infidel or Atheist."**

> "Some Books against deism fell into my hands; they were said to be the Substance of Sermons preached at Boyle's Lectures. It happened that they wrought an Effect on me quite contrary to what was intended by them: For the Arguments of the Deists which were quoted to be refuted, appeared to me much stronger than the Refutations. In short I became a thorough Deist."

"I early absented myself from the Public Assemblies of the Sect (Presbyterian). Sunday being my studying-Days". Concerning this church attendance "My conduct might be blameable, but I leave it without attempting farther to excuse it". All of these religious stances seem mild unless one was brought up in a family and Community which strictly adhered to them, and expected others to do the same. In this atmo-

Chapter 7: Independence

sphere it was rebellion to hold views radically different from the established system and would definitely earn the title of "Infidel". To stand thus, a man must have confidence in his opinions and in himself. He must be able to hold onto ideas which only he can defend while others attack. He must be strong enough to stand alone on the inside and to be his own best counsel. A man must most literally be independent. Such men are a threat to established ways, but they are also the seeds of growth. From these come the new structures, ideas, and tools that change the world and make it a better place. Had Franklin been less independent or less willful he may have been anonymous to history. His place would be with those who followed the path laid by others. He would have believed something only after a new Sect had been formed by other intellectual pioneers. If a man cannot believe something for himself and by himself, he cannot be anything but one of the faceless masses, and this Benjamin Franklin was not.

In business Franklin was not cast into the apprenticeship and lifetime trade mold. He ran away from his brother's master-ship. Then, seeing better opportunity as a merchant than as a printer he changed professions. And later when his merchant sponsor died, he again returned to the printing business. Often his mind cut against the ways of the current society. When criticized in his plans to form a subscription library he stood by his own opinion and was proven right. At printing houses he refused to partake in the customary drink. Though a bit ostracized for it, he was able to earn a place in their company based on his uniqueness rather than his conformity.

Upon becoming the comptroller of the Post Master General of America he instituted changes in order to make it a profitable, self-sustaining venture, not what it had previously been.

"The American Office had never hitherto paid anything to that of Britain. We were to have 600 pounds a Year between us if we could make that sum out of the Profits of the Office. To do this, a Variety of Improvements were necessary; some of these were inevitably at first expensive; so that in the first four Years the Office became above 900 pounds in debt to us. But it soon after began to repay us, and before I was displac'd, by a Freak of the Minister's, of which I shall speak hereafter, we had brought it to yield three times as much clear Revenue to the Crown as the Post-Office of Ireland. Since that imprudent Transaction, they have receiv'd from it—not one Farthing."

This enterprise shows the man's ingenuity and faith in his ideas. Without this he could have scarce waited to earn back his investment of four years.

INDEPENDENCE:

An aversion to arbitrary power has stuck to me thrò my whole life.

AGREEABLE

THROUGHOUT HIS Autobiography Benjamin Franklin recommends an agreeable manner with one's fellows and a certain avoidance of disputation. His many friendships and their positive effect on his fortune probably owes much to this manner of handling them. A friend argued against, may quickly become a friend on the exterior while inside an opponent. Thus an argumentative nature loses more battles than it wins.

As a young man Franklin speaks of his friend Collins, "We sometimes disputed, and very fond we were of Argument, & very desirous of confuting one another. Which disputatious Turn, by the way, is apt to become a very bad Habit, making People often extremely disagreeable in Company, by the Contradiction that is necessary to bring it into Practice, & thence, besides souring & spoiling the Conversation, is productive of Disgusts & perhaps Enmities

Franklin, in his fur hat, charmed the French with what they saw as rustic new world genius.

CHAPTER
8

were you may have occasion for Friendship." So he learned from his behavior that the course he was embarked upon held an ill future and was best changed to one of an agreeable nature.

He speaks with the same opinion of disputation during his later life in advice to the new English Governor of the colonies. The old governor had resigned, **"tir'd with the Disputes his Proprietary Instructions subjected him to"**. It appears that arguing with the representatives of the colonies had worn him out. The new governor asked Franklin if he could expect as uncomfortable a time as his predecessor. Franklin answered **"No; you may on the contrary have a very comfortable one, if you will only take care not to enter into any Dispute with the Assembly."** Governor Morris' reply **"My dear Friend ... how can you advise my avoiding Disputes. You know I love Disputing; it is one of my greatest pleasures; However, to show the Regard I have for your Counsel, I promise you I will if possible avoid them."** But he did not avoid them, but began the practice immediately. Franklin himself wrote most of the answers to Gov. Morris' arguments and soon Morris **"grew tir'd of the Contest, and quitted the Government"**.

Franklin says that Morris **"had some Reason for loving to dispute, being eloquent, an acute Sophister, and therefore generally successful in argumentative Conversation."** Though Franklin's advice is against using this skill, **"But I think the Practice was not wise, for in the Course of my Observation, those disputing, contradicting & confuting People are generally unfortunate in their Affairs. They get Victory sometimes, but they never get Good Will, which would be of more use to them."**

The getting of goodwill is much more profitable in the long run than the winning of arguments. Though winning may yield an immediate victory and its spoils, goodwill plants the seed which yields much more fruit over time. Benjamin Franklin exhibited this characteristic as a young man in a London printing house. He thought it unfair to pay dues for ale which he would not drink. After several weeks he found that his fellows performed mischief on him and his work and he therefore paid the dues "convinc'd of the Folly of being on ill Terms with those one is to live with continually. I was now on a fair footing with them, and soon acquir'd considerable Influence."

In dealing with the church we have learned that he was not a strong philosophical supporter, but still contributed financially. **"Tho' I seldom attended any Public Worship, I had still an Opinion of its Propriety, and of its Utility when rightly conducted, and I regularly paid my annual Subscription for the Support of the only Presbyterian Minister or Meeting we had in Philadelphia."** And again **"I quitted the Congregation, never joining it after, tho' I continu'd many Years my Subscription for the Support of its Ministers"**. This behavior could be called hypocritical by those who like to judge all situations as black or white. Or it could be considered wise in view of the circumstances. Franklin had chosen to separate himself from the dominant religious persuasion of the time. This offense would be made more grievous by his refusal to support the church monetarily. Thus, by his support he acknowledged the value of the work and his partnership with it. He also redeemed some of his reputation and therefore could not be treated as a complete heathen, since such people not being preferred for business and social relations.

Franklin desired to be on good terms with men whom he lived around, and especially those forming the new colonies. As a member of the General Assembly he was quite successful. In 1736 he was again proposed as a Clerk of the assembly but a new member made a long Speech against him, and in favor of another. Even though Franklin was chosen for the position he desired to be on good terms with this critic. He **"did not like the Opposition of this new Member, who was a Gentleman of Fortune, & Education, with Talents that were likely to give him in time great Influence in the House, which indeed afterwards happened. I did not however aim at gaining his Favor by paying any servile Respect to him, but after some time took this other Method. Having heard that he had in his Library a certain very scarce & curious Book, I wrote a Note to him expressing my Desire of perusing that Book, and requesting he would do** me the Favor of lending it to me for a few Days. He sent it immediately; and I return'd it in about a Week, with another Note expressing strongly my Sense of the Favor. When we next met in the House he spoke to me, (which he had never done before) and with great Civility. And he ever afterwards manifested a Readiness to serve me on all Occasions, so that we became great Friends, & our Friendship continu'd to his Death."

Again in Philadelphia he was instrumental in creating forces for the general defense. A "Dr. B" ascribed much of the credit to himself and Franklin comments "I had the Vanity to ascribe all to my Dialogue; However, not knowing but that he might be in the right, I let him enjoy his Opinion, which I take to be generally the best way in such Cases." We wonder how a man so willing to let credit for his work slip into the hands of other men was ever able to be so powerful and well recognized in the formation of the country. Perhaps the credit was never taken by another in the eyes of the community. Though another man's name may appear next to an idea or accomplishment, the truth will be known generally. Americans gave him respect for his contributions, a commodity more valuable than money.

Lastly, when Franklin's papers on his electrical experiments were published they met with much criticism. In Europe professional societies and scientific men of note disagreed openly with his theories. Chief among them was **"The Count de Buffon, a philosopher deservedly of great Reputation in France"**. This man had his own theories of electricity which disagreed with Franklin's. He therefore produced a volume of letters defending his theories and denying Franklin's. At first Franklin was inclined to answer these criticisms but after considering it—"I concluded to let my Papers shift for themselves; believing it was better to spend what time I could spare from public Business in making new Experiments, than in Disputing about those already made. I therefore never answer'd M. Nollet; and the Event gave me no Cause to repent my Silence".

With this attitude Franklin was free to investigate fields and create new inventions with his time and energy. Today we associate one

Chapter 8: Agreeable

name with the discovery of electricity and no one knows the theories of Count de Buffon.

AGREEABLE:

Convinc'd of the folly of being on ill terms with those one is to live with continually.

HUMILITY

AS FRANKLIN was an exceptional man he was also a proud man, successful in business, politics, writing, and inventing. "But a Quaker Friend having kindly inform'd me that I was generally thought proud; that my Pride show'd itself frequently in Conversation; That I was not content with being in the right when discussing any Point, but was overbearing & rather insolent; of which he convinc'd me by mentioning several Instances; I determined endeavoring to cure myself if I could of this Vice or Folly among the rest, and I added Humility to my Lot, giving an extensive Meaning to the Word. I cannot boast of much Success in acquiring the Reality of this Virtue; but I had a good deal with regard to the Appearance of it."

His pride was acknowledged a vice and he endeavored to replace it with humility. Being a business man and involved

Franklin was the Postmaster General of Philadelphia in 1737 and one of two Postmaster Generals of North America in 1753.

CHAPTER
9

in public service he could ill afford to offend his patrons with his pride. This he must conquer—but he could not. Rather it was covered, creating the appearance of Humility. In relations with men this will suffice to free you of the problems that come with pride. You will, therefore, go on more pleasantly in Your affairs and will meet with more success. Your projects will be accepted and friends will be more willing to instruct you in improvement. A proud man who has arrived at perfection will most often be left to his delusion and will not benefit from the wisdom of his neighbors.

Being a man of public spirit and project He soon found the dividends of humility.

> "The Objections, & Reluctances I met with in Soliciting the Subscriptions (for a library), made me soon feel the Impropriety of presenting one's self as the Proposer of any useful Project that might be suppos'd to raise one's Reputation in the smallest degree above that of one's Neighbors, when one has need of their Assistance to accomplish that Project. I therefore put myself as much as I could out of sight, and stated it as a Scheme of a Number of Friends, who had requested me to go about and propose it to such as they thought Lovers of Reading. In this way my Affair went on more smoothly, and I ever after practis'd it on such Occasions; and from my frequent successes, can heartily recommend it. The present little Sacrifice of your Vanity will afterwards be amply repaid. If it remains a while uncertain to whom the Merit belongs, some one more vain then yourself will be encourag'd to claim it, and even then Envy will be dispos'd to do you Justice, by plucking those assum'd Feathers & restoring them to their right Owner".

Then again when proposing that an academy be built for the education of the youth—"In the introduction to these Proposals, I stated their Publication not as an Act of mine, but of some public-spirited Gentleman; avoiding as much as I could, according to my usual Rule, The presenting myself to the Public as the Author of any Scheme for their Benefit."

Chapter 9: Humility

Just as with his agreeable attitude in dealing with others we find this humility a seed for future fruit. The man who is responsible for good will generally be found out, and the reward freely bestowed upon him. But a proud man, eager for a reputation will find his plans blocked by his peers, and credit given at best grudgingly. Franklin's proverbs of planning for the future **"A penny saved is a penny earned"**, etc. apply equally to the conduct of ones ego. The self-conquered ego will find itself lifted up and enthroned. The self-congratulatory ego will find itself pulled down and trampled upon. Many today feel it imperative to promote themselves and collect glory openly. They fear that another will get that which they have rightly earned, and so they turn to ignoble methods and statements to avoid losing their right. If their mind were more concerned with the good of the project and its success they would have less concern for themselves. Glory would then be free to settle about the shoulders of the deserving party rather than being pursued. Perhaps we spend our energy on so few worthy projects and so many monotonous ones that we fear that the little real reward available will be lost. In this case the solution is not glory hunting, but rather a redirection of effort. We must focus on projects worthy of our energy and let others fall undone by the way-side. This would increase our productivity, self-esteem, and value and decrease our frustrations, emptiness, and futility. This is a change for long term success rather than daily acknowledgement of doing the right thing.

Franklin made wise, but humble decisions on other circumstances. Finding his efforts to organize forces for the common defense—**"The Officers of the Companies composing the Philadelphia Regiment, being met, chose me for their Colonel; but conceiving myself unfit, I declin'd that station, & recommended Mr. Lawrence, a fine Person and Man of Influence, who was accordingly appointed."** Though he was not appointed here he was later made Colonel of another Regiment. When he departed from this post the men were determined to honor his service. They mounted in uniform with swords drawn to escort him out of town **"I had not been** previously acquainted with the Project, or I should have prevented it, being naturally averse to the assuming of State on any Occasion".

Franklin believed this to be an important virtue and thus endeavors to inculcate it. His failure to succeed may indicate a greater degree of humility than he realized he possessed.

"In reality there is perhaps no one of our natural Passions so hard to subdue as Pride. Disguise it, struggle with it, beat it down, stifle it, mortify it as much as one pleases, it is still alive, and will every now and then peep out and show itself."

HUMILITY:

Immodest Words admit but this Defense, That Want of Modesty is Want of Sense.

CHARACTER

BENJAMIN FRANKLIN valued "good" moral character. He endeavored to behave honorably and to strengthen his own all through life. During a time of reflection he says, "I grew convinc'd that Truth, Sincerity & Integrity in Dealings between Man & Man, were of the utmost Importance to the Felicity of Life, and I form'd written Resolutions, (which still remain in my Journal Book) to practice them ever while I lived." He also says, "I had therefore a tolerable Character to begin the World with, I valued it properly, & determin'd to preserve it."

Rather than a vague notion of trying to be good he drew up a plan. This consisted of a list of the characteristics of an exemplary man. There were:

1) Temperance
2) Silence
3) Order

Franklin's Pennsylvania Gazette, Sept 25, 1729.

CHAPTER
10

4) Resolution	9) Moderation
5) Frugality	10) Cleanliness
6) Industry	11) Tranquility
7) Sincerity	12) Chastity
8) Justice	13) Humility.

To improve these characteristics he had a method. This was to create a table with the days of the week across the top and the characteristics down the side. Each week he focused his attention on one item. He endeavored to commit no offenses against that item during that week. This practice being like exercise would strengthen that characteristic and make him a better man. The next week he would move to the next item. This practice he kept up for some years showing his sincerity at obtaining a strong moral character. Though he did not claim to have perfected himself with this exercise he did feel that it strengthened him and left him a better man than he would have been had he not done it.

We have seen his independent spirit in choosing his religious beliefs. But aside from practicing as he saw fit he sought no conflicts with other religions. He felt of other religions "... **Respect to all, with an Opinion that the worst had some good Effects, induc'd me to avoid all Discourse that might tend to lessen the good Opinion another might have of his own Religion**".

Character was not a suit of clothes which could be donned at convenient times and doffed at others. It was a part of his existence, what he was rather than what he did. Therefore, his conduct was the same in business and personal matters.

When offered money by friends to start his own business venture by breaking off with his current partner "**I told them I could not propose a Separation while any Prospect remain'd of the Merediths fulfilling their Part of our Agreement. Because I thought myself under great Obligations to them for what they had done & would do if they could**".

When he did at last start his own business he had the habit of paying his debt. "**I began now gradually to pay off the Debt I was under for the Printing house.**" And "**Thus being esteem'd an industrious thriving young**

Man, and paying duly for what I bought, the Merchants who imported stationery solicited my Custom". This habit of paying ones debts is extremely important. A man willing to extend you credit has placed a trust in your hands. And it is only by honest character that you are bound to pay the debt you accrue. If you do not you have shattered a trust and will find it very difficult to deal with him or others in his sphere again. By taking goods or money and not repaying it you threaten another's business. And in threatening his business you threaten his family in that he will not be able to feed and cloth them if all customers behave as you have. Franklin values this so much that he records the following story in his autobiography as an illustration of an exemplary man.

"I must record one Trait of this good Man's Character. He had formerly been in Business at Bristol, but fail'd in Debt to a Number of People, compounded and went to America. There, by close Application to Business as a Merchant, he acquir'd a plentiful Fortune in a few Years. Returning to England in the ship with me, He invited his old Creditors to an Entertainment, at which he thank'd them for the easy Composition they had favor'd him with, & when they expected nothing but the Treat, every Man at the first Remove, found under his plate an Order on a Banker for the full Amount of the unpaid Remainder with Interest."

As a new printer Franklin found that one of the older printers was also the post master. In that position the man took advantage and refused to let Franklin send his newspapers through the post. This would have lost Franklin much money had he not solved the problem by bribing the post riders to take his newspapers privately. Some years later Franklin himself became the post master. But he did not behave this way toward other men's newspaper businesses as it was not in keeping with honest practices.

Later when Franklin invented the Pennsylvania Fire Place (a.k.a. the Franklin stove) he had the opportunity to patent the idea and make quite a bit of money from it. The Governor **"offer'd to give me a Patent** for the sole Vending of them for a Term of Years; but I declin'd it from a Principle which has ever weigh'd with me on such Occasions, viz. That as we enjoy great Advantages from the Inventions of others, we should be glad of an Opportunity to serve others by any Invention of ours, and this we should do freely and generously." Today it may seem amazing that he would forgo a small fortune for such a principle. But to him the money made in accordance with principle was enough and that without principle was too much. In fact another man from London did patent the stove and made a little fortune on it.

It is clear that in the 13 points he has enumerated Benjamin Franklin's character was exemplary. He set his moral goals and strove to reach them throughout his life. For this he was a better man and today we remember him as a great man. Finally Franklin recounts this story:

> "Like the Man who in buying an Ax of a Smith my Neighbor, desired to have the whole of its Surface as bright as the Edge; the Smith consented to grind it bright for him if he would turn the Wheel. He Turn'd while the Smith press'd the broad Face of the Ax hard and heavily on the stone, which made the Turning of it very fatiguing. The Man came every now & then from the Wheel to see how the Work went on; and at length would take his Ax as it was without farther Grinding. No says the Smith, Turn on, turn on; we shall have it bright by and by; as yet 'tis only speckled. Yes, says the Man, but—I think I like a speckled Ax best. And I believe this may have been the Case with many who having for want of some such Means as I employ'd found the Difficulty of obtaining good, & breaking bad Habits, in other Points of Vice & Virtue, have given up the Struggle, & concluded that a speckled Ax was best."

CHARACTER:

Truth, Sincerity & Integrity in Dealings between Man & Man, were of the utmost Importance to the Felicity of Life.

HONESTY

BEN FRANKLIN was known as an honest man. He showed his honesty in business and personal matters as do many good men. But he also displays an honesty with himself, of his weaknesses and mistakes he does not make excuses or seek to place blame on others, rather he accepts responsibility for his own actions and their consequences.

From the beginning of the autobiography he admits to one motive for writing it. "And lastly, (I may as well confess it, since my Denial of it will be believ'd by nobody) perhaps I shall a good deal gratify my own Vanity. Indeed I scarce ever heard or saw the introductory Words, Without Vanity I may say, &c but some vain thing immediately follow'd." If a man cannot be honest in viewing himself he certainly can not present himself to others as an honest man. His reputation

A marble statue of Benjamin Franklin stands in the atrium of Benjamin Franklin High School in New Orleans, Louisiana.

CHAPTER
11

for honesty must begin as honesty with himself.

In dealing with his indenture to his brother he admitted to taking advantage of the situation and that he erred in his behavior. "It was not fair of me to take this Advantage, and this I therefore reckon one of the first Errata of my Life". Then again when spending money belonging to another, "The Breaking into this money of Vernon's was one of the first great Errata of my Life. And this Affair show'd that my Father was not much out in his Judgement when he suppos'd me too Young to manage Business of Importance." Concerning his fiance in America while in England, "... Miss Read, to whom I never wrote more than one Letter, & that was to let her know I was not likely soon to return. This was another of the great Errata of my Life, which I should wish to correct if I were to live it over again." These "errata" he freely admitted and accepted the responsibility for. In fact, all three were redeemed, as much as was possible, by his later actions. He was able to look at himself and see honestly what was inside. Without this can any man be truly great? Indeed he may soar to the top of society but then just as quickly plummet to the bottom. To remain on top and growing one must see oneself with clear eyes. Our faults must be accepted and treated as opportunities for improvement. If they are covered up they will only ferment, growing larger and more nauseous. He who can expose and address his problems will more likely heal them and become a stronger man. He will then be prepared to successfully meet the larger challenges in life and to conquer them.

Later, Franklin speaks of his situation at the age of 23. "In the mean time, that hard-to-be-govern'd Passion of Youth, had hurried me frequently into Intrigues with low Women that fell in my Way, which were attended with some Expense & great Inconvenience, besides a continual Risk to my Health by a Distemper which of all Things I dreaded, tho' by great gook Luck I escaped it." He honestly admitted to sexual impropriety. This is amazing considering that it was written in 1771 and addressed to his son. In that time such behavior can not have been accepted by society and he risked extreme embarrassment of his public reputation. These facts are being shared with his son as a way of instruction, to speak so honestly was certainly a risk to encouraging like behavior. He must have felt highly the importance of honesty to have included this passage.

> "In 1736 I lost one of my Sons, a fine Boy of 4 Years old, by the Small Pox taken in the common way. I long regretted bitterly & still regret that I had not given it to him by Inoculation; this I mention for the Sake of Parents, who omit that Operation on the Supposition that they should never forgive themselves if a Child died under it; my Example showing that the Regret may be the same either way, and that therefore the safer should be chosen."

A mistake made which cost the life of his son. Surely he could have ascribed this to the medical profession or the lack of knowledge of the time. But he accepted the responsibility and carried it heavily all through his life. What befell him was not someone else's fault but rather his own—his to learn from, grow from, and never to repeat.

HONESTY:

An honest man is the noblest work of God.

ENTERPRISING

BEFORE STRIKING OUT on his own as a printer Franklin detoured into the profession of merchant. While a hired hand at a print shop he compared it with the opportunity being offered by a merchant acquaintance. The man, Mr. Denham, offered Franklin a position in keeping his books with the opportunity to advance to a merchant himself. **"Therefore, I immediately agreed, on the Terms of Fifty Pounds a Year, Pennsylvania Money; less indeed than my present Gettings as a Compositor, but affording a better Prospect."** He saw himself not as a printer bound to the profession for life but as a free man. He was ready to seize opportunity and become what that opportunity could make him. This flexible attitude helped him become a success since he was not limited by others' ideas but could grow to any stature which his

The Franklin Stove.

CHAPTER
TWELVE

own mind and skills could maintain. Franklin did not remain a merchant long as his sponsor died, putting an end to the position. But he was left a small legacy and returned to printing at **"an Offer of large Wages"**.

This increase in wages is a common factor when changing jobs. One will find that he has been undervalued at his former employer. He may have been hired as a junior man but as his expertise grew the position and pay did not grow proportionately. Perhaps there is no position for him or more likely the employer can not view a man with objective eyes but rather sees him as the man he once was. In the same way a parent sees a son as a child long after he has grown into a man. Thus, experience and continual education is profitable, though not through the devotion of oneself to a single master.

Franklin soon had his own print house and performed several actions which made it a superior establishment to that of his competitors. One of these ideas was this, "... **Bradford still printed the Votes & Laws & other Public Business. He had printed an Address of the House to the Governor in a course blundering manner; We reprinted it elegantly & correctly, and sent one to every Member. They were sensible of the Difference, it strengthen'd the Hands of our Friends in the House, and they voted us their Printers for the Year ensuing.**" This was an investment, in many ways an advertisement. Rather than speaking with the members of the House and attempting to persuade them to give him their business, he boldly showed them his superior work. This can not have been taken kindly by Bradford though it was by the House. Words are very empty compared to acts such as these. There could be no doubt that Franklin's work was superior. It may be that he recognized the fact that it was important to the body representing the new colonies to put on an impressive face in dealing with the British government, and that this face was most clearly shown in written materials passing from the one to the other. In this Franklin recognized a customer's need and filled it without being asked. How could the House know that their correspondence could be more professionally rendered by a printer? They were

Chapter 12: Enterprising

not in the profession and did not know what level of quality they may have asked for.

As mentioned earlier this same Bradford was in charge of the post office. In that position he refused to let Franklin send his newspapers through the mail. To remedy this Franklin took to bribing the riders privately to carry his newspapers and thus kept his circulation up. Later when Franklin became the Philadelphia deputy to the Post-Master General, **"I accepted it readily, and found it of great Advantage; for tho' the Salary was small, it facilitated the Correspondence that improv'd my Newspaper, increas'd the Number demanded, as well as the Advertisements to be inserted, so that it came to afford me a very considerable Income."** Thus public office did then, as it does now, provide opportunity to profit. This is one reason Lawyers and Doctors can be found serving the community in many different affairs. In addition to their civic duty it is a form of business enhancement.

Franklin mentions two other posts which also provided business opportunity. The first was as Clerk of the General Assembly, **"As besides the pay for immediate Service as Clerk, the Place gave me a better Opportunity of keeping up on Interest among the Members, which secur'd to me the Business of Printing the votes, Laws, Paper Money, and other occasional Jobs for the Public, that on the whole were very profitable."** This business came out of the hands of his competitor Bradford, who seems to be losing customers on all fronts to the young Benjamin Franklin.

At the end of the Autobiography he speaks of representing the colonies to the British government. He says **"The Assembly look'd on my entering into the first Part of the Engagement as an essential Service to the Province, since it secur'd the Credit of the Paper Money then spread over all the Country; and they gave me their Thanks in form when I return'd."** It seems his services were rewarded with the very money he went to defend. This service was a benefit to the whole country and thus it is not unseemly that he should be rewarded in some way. Such good help can not be taken for free and remain long available for future use.

Something that all successful business men know and that Franklin practiced, he must "**often receive People of Business at their own Hours.**" This requires personal flexibility and a devotion to the success of your venture. Without this a man may seem undependable or uninterested in conducting business seriously. When running your own business you will find that a normal working day has twenty-four hours din it rather than eight. To work with others you will find yourself laboring late into the night, meeting over dinner, and conducting business in the early morning when other men are still asleep. This devotion must be real, but it also should be visible. As Franklin was seen working late into the night and taking work home in a wheel-barrow, you too must have a reputation for working as hard as is required to get the job done.

Franklin established partnerships with his best employees. These he set up with print houses of their own, providing equipment in exchange for a portion of the revenue. This turned hired hands into business owners and thus provided a better life for many families. Though such partnerships often ended in failure, Franklin's succeeded. The reasons he gives are as follows. "**Partnerships often finish in Quarrels, but I was happy in this, that mine were all carry'd on and ended amicably; owing I think a good deal to the Precautions of having very explicitly settled in our Articles every thing to be done by or expected from each Partner, so that there was nothing to dispute, which Precaution I would therefore recommend to all who enter into Partnerships, for whatever Esteem Partners may have for & Confidence in each other at the time of the Contract, little Jealousies and Disgusts may arise, with Ideas of Inequality in the Care & Burden of the Business, which are attended often with Breach of Friendship & of the Connection, perhaps with Lawsuits and other disagreeable Consequences.**" Through these partnerships Franklin was able to increase the availability of printing to the colonists, establish families in business, and increase his own estate.

Franklin has advice for all men. Advice that is intended to make a poor Man's fortune. "**And I should from this Circumstance, there be-**

ing always in the world a Number of rich Merchants, Nobility, States and Princes, who have need of honest Instruments for the Management of their Affairs, and such being so rare have endeavored to convince young Persons, that no Qualities were so likely to make a poor Man's Fortune as those of Probity & Integrity." The most important characteristic for making your fortune is not one of birth, not of education, not of physical ability, and not of position. It is of primary importance that a man have integrity. Thus all men are in a position to begin the journey of success.

Once you have begun you will find an ally to aid you as Franklin did. "I experienc'd too the Truth of the Observation, that after getting the first hundred Pound, it is more easy to get the second: Money itself being of a prolific Nature."

ENTERPRISING:
Drive thy business, let not that drive thee.

OPTIMISTIC

ALL MEN HAVE opinions about life and the circumstances there in. They either have confidence in these ideas or think them no more that a wisp of thought, believing instead that the opinions of others are more worthy of respect. The second are the ultimate followers, the servants of other men, and the hands of another's brain. Franklin was not of this temper. He stood by his projects in the face of criticism and reaped rewards while others remained poor.

He provided an excellent example of this. "...there are Croakers in every Country always boding its ruin. Such a one then lived in Philadelphia, a Person of Note, an elderly Man, with a wise Look, and a very grave Manner of speaking. His Name was Samuel Mickle. This Gentleman, a Stranger to me, stopped one Day at my Door, and asked me if I was the young Man who had lately open'd a new

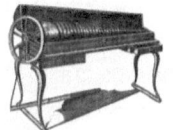

Among Franklin's many creations was the glass harmonica.

CHAPTER
13

Printing-house; being answer'd in the Affirmative he said he was sorry for me, because it was an expensive Undertaking & the Expense would be lost; for Philadelphia was a sinking Place. The People already half Bankrupt or near being so; all Appearances of the contrary, such as new Buildings & the Rise of Rents being to his certain Knowledge fallacious, for they were in fact among the Things that would soon ruin us. And he gave me such a Detail of Misfortunes, now existing or that were soon to exist, that he left me half-melancholy. Had I known him before I engag'd in this Business, probably I never should have done it. This man continu'd to live in this decaying Place, and to remain in the same strain, refusing for many Years to buy a house there, because all was going to Destruction, and at last I had the Pleasure of seeing him give five times as much for one as he might have bought it for when he first began his Croaking."

Had Franklin been overly persuaded by this man we may not have had one of our greatest citizens. Notice that the "Croaker" was—a person of note—an elderly man—with a wise look—and a very grave manner of speaking. On the surface all the qualities of knowledge and wisdom. He was armed with the tools to make his words strong and effective. Unfortunately these tools were used to discourage enterprise and growth. Many young, eager men will come across such elders. Those men have helped to make society and business what it is today. Their brains and sweat are responsible for the situation a young man begins with. These elders are to be respected for their own experience and knowledge but beware their view of the future. Tomorrow will be better, more advanced and more replete with opportunity as long as men are willing to work toward growth. If an old man croaks about the end of progress he has been blinded by his own age. Do not heed negative, down beat forebodings about the future, it is a bright place of great potential just waiting to be built.

Another questionable circumstance is that this man did not know Franklin at all. The elder sought him out to deliver the dire news of Philadelphia's destruction for some strange reason. Perhaps he just enjoyed hearing his own words or seeing their effect on innocent subjects. It is also possible that this man's "friends" had received all of this tripe they could stand and no longer listened to him, thus forcing him to seek new ears for his preaching.

If Philadelphia was so wretched then what was he doing there? Why does he not leave to improve his fortune? He is still there because he is in the business of Croaking and has no other to preserve or give attention to. For those who croak and those who listen the world is indeed a terrible place which continually abuses them. For proof they can point to the fact that they paid five times the just price for their house. To those who see the world more positively it is a place of reward and opportunity. They are so busy taking opportunity and reaping the reward that they cannot pause to entertain the croakers.

Franklin conceived of a scheme for improving the morality of the country. It was an enormous task which he never had the opportunity to begin. But he states, "**I was not discourag'd by the seeming magnitude of the undertaking, as I have always thought that one Man of tolerable Abilities may work great Changes, & accomplish great Affairs among Mankind, if he first forms a good Plan, and, cutting off all Amusements or other Employments that would divert his Attention, makes the Execution of that same Plan his sole Study and Business.**" Any scheme no matter how large or great must first begin with one man's mind and muscle. Individuals are the catalyst and womb of all great enterprises and no change occurs except when a single man takes action. We have lost some of the confidence in individuals that Franklin and his revolutionary companions had. We believe rather that governments, committees, and corporations are the incubators of great enterprises. This is false. It is only individuals in these organizations that create great things. Individuals anywhere can do the same.

He displayed his solid confidence several times in the Autobiography:

> "A young Gentleman who had likewise some Friends in the House, and wished to succeed me as their Clerk, acquainted me that it was decided to displace me at the next Election, and he

therefore in Good Will advis'd me to resign, as more consistent with my Honor than being turn'd out. My Answer to him was, that I had read or heard of some Public Man, who made it a Rule never to ask for an Office, and never to refuse one when offer'd to him. I approve, says I, of this Rule, and will practise it with a small Addition; I shall l never ask, never refuse, nor ever resign an Office... I was chosen again, unanimously as usual, at the next Election."

After Franklin wrote of his electrical experiments the paper was read by many members of the Royal Society in England, "**who wrote me word that it had been read but was laughed at by the Connoisseurs**". This Society was composed of some of the most learned men in the world—they were absolutely wrong and Franklin was right. A man can be just as wrong when he has credentials as when he has none. The then unknown Franklin, though right, had to stand alone with his theories against the established intelligence of the day. This required confidence and strength from within.

Later when debating the royal jurisdiction over the colonies Franklin had to stand against established power again. The British representative argued that they could make laws over the colonies and Franklin maintained that they could not. The other "**assur'd me I was totally mistaken. I did not think so however. And his Lordship's conversation having a little alarm'd me as to what might be the Sentiments of the Court concerning us, I wrote it down as soon as I return'd to my Lodgings.**" When opposed by a stronger power he did not buckle but rather prepared to defend his position with greater strength.

Always strong against strong opposition Franklin proved that the individual is supreme over all institutions. Institutions hold firmly the present but only individuals can build and explore the future.

OPTIMISTIC:

Do not anticipate trouble, or worry about what may never happen. Keep in the sunlight.

TRAVEL

FRANKLIN'S FREE spirit and hard work resulted in opportunities for him to travel at a young age. At seventeen he had moved from his native Boston to New York and Philadelphia. In Philadelphia he went to work as a printer and soon earned a respectable sum. In a mere seven months he was able to return home, **"having a genteel new suit from Head to foot, a Watch, and my Pockets lin'd with near Five Pounds Sterling in silver."** What did he think of this new country that provided so well for him? **"I prais'd it much, & the happy Life I led in it; expressing strongly my Intention of returning to it"**.

Benjamin Franklin, Ambassador to France (1776-1789).

We often get used to the home we have and fear to leave it for unknown country. This fear holds us in place and traps us in our current situation. When a man has grown up in an area he has a life-time of baggage and expectations hanging about

CHAPTER
14

him. These have been forming all through his life and intend to define his future. If he desires to be more than this image he must fight ferociously to escape and may never succeed. He is always that young man who did those irresponsible things in his youth and is not quite ready for serious responsibility. His history forms a straight jacket that prohibits growth and success.

The most sure way to break these bonds is to move and leave that unwanted baggage behind. In a new place you are now an unknown and must be defined by your current stature rather than your past. Here you can be who you want and do as you dare. It is the time to cast off the person you have been cloaked as by others and to be that which glows within your soul. Because of Franklin's move he is no longer an apprentice tied behind his brother and following where he leads. His accomplishments now reside within himself and he need not wait on one man to allow him to be what he is or desires. Franklin is now free to attach himself where he pleases and to study from those that can help him the most. These men will see him as a free man, able to set his own destiny, rather than a bound servant at their disposal.

Aside from his new belongings Franklin returned from Philadelphia with a letter from that colony's Governor to his father. This letter recommended Benjamin as a fine worker and proposed setting him up with his own print shop. This situation was far superior to anything Franklin could have hoped for had he stayed in Boston. The effect of this letter must have been to raise the senior Franklin's opinion of his son and more importantly to raise Benjamin's opinion of himself. This self-concept in every man receives a great boost when others think so highly. Events such as these serve to build the man beyond his own expectations and begin his launch into great accomplishments. Without these boosts a man may never really have confidence in what he is and what he thinks. This may leave him lolling about in an average life where dreams are never more solid than mist. As one would expect Mr. Franklin did not approve of the plan. He could not see Benjamin as

CHAPTER 14: TRAVEL

more than the young, saucy man that he watched grow from a child. Although wishing the best for his son, as all fathers do, he would provide him with opportunity much after the younger was able to handle it. Thus stunting his growth and making him more like his ancestors than he should be.

From Philadelphia Franklin goes to England. Not entirely on his own boldness but on the promise of the governor to set him up as a printer. These promises and his support turn out to be empty vessels and Franklin finds himself alone and without employment in London. He went to work at established print shops and learned more about the trade than he ever could have in America. This knowledge and experience served him profitably throughout his life. Since the trade was much more advanced in England than in the New World, Franklin acquired skills that were rare or non-existent in America. Upon his return these skills made him a valuable man and he was able to sell his services at double the prices of his fellow American printers. These were also the tools which enabled him to make a print shop of his own and to guide it to greater success than all the others in Philadelphia. His standard of quality was set by what he saw in England which is far superior to that being produced in America.

Thus moving to new places transforms a man. This is half by what it does to him and half by what is releases him from. The experience, freedom, and confidence instilled by travel cannot be duplicated in any other way. It is essential that a man "see the world" if he hopes to be great and successful. Conquering the fear of the unknown will begin a process of growth that will not stop as long as that fear is not allowed to return to control.

TRAVEL:
You may delay, but time will not.

CHARITY

FRANKLIN ACCOMPLISHED much toward his personal success but he also contributed greatly to the advancement of the Colonies. He was a giving man who was eager to aid progress through his personal abilities and influence. In America many of the institutions of society did not yet exist and people were so busy providing for their own needs that few had time to help develop them. But Benjamin Franklin saw these as public needs and addressed himself to them. At the age of 24, **"And now I set on foot my first project of a public Nature, that for a Subscription Library. I drew up the Proposals, got them put into Form by our great Scrivener Brockden, and by the help of my Friends in the Junto, procur'd Fifty subscribers of 40/ each to begin with & 10/ a Year for 50 years, the Term our company was to continue. We afterwards obtain'd a Charter, the Company

John Trumbull depicts the Committee of Five that drafted the Declaration of Independence.

CHAPTER
15

being increas'd to 100. This was the mother of all the North American Subscription Libraries now so numerous. It is become a great thing itself, & continually increasing. These Libraries have improv'd the general Conversation of the Americans, made the common Tradesmen & Farmers as intelligent as most Gentlemen from other Countries, and perhaps have contributed in some degree to the stand so generally made throughout the colonies in Defense of their Privileges."

It should not surprise us that his first project involved books and learning—two of Franklin's greatest loves. Thus we see that the interests of one man can cause him to produce an institution which benefits an entire community. And this learning received by the Americans may have contributed to the successful uprising known as the American Revolution.

This is only the first in a series of public services spearheaded by Franklin. He also addressed the City Watch, a form of Police force. These were charging a flat rate to all citizens for their protective services regardless of a person's wealth. Franklin defended the position that each person should pay according to the value of the property being protected, thus assessing the greatest cost to those who benefitted the most by the service.

He also wrote a paper which outlined the need and form of a Fire company. This secured many houses from being totally destroyed by fire and saved others by dousing the flames before they spread to neighboring buildings. He thought through and articulated the specific requirements of the Fire company and the equipment it needed.

> "I had on the whole abundant Reason to be satisfied with my being established in Pennsylvania. There were however two things that I regretted: there being no Provision for Defense, nor for a complete Education of Youth; No militia nor any College. I, therefore in 1743, drew up a Proposal for establishing an Academy."

Then known as the University of Philadelphia, it is now the University of Pennsylvania. Franklin, "**had the very great Pleasure of seeing a Number**

Chapter 15: Charity

of the Youth who have receiv'd their Education in it, distinguish'd by their improv'd Abilities, serviceable in public Stations, and Ornaments to their Country".

A later paper described the need for a local defense against the French and the Indians. This resulted in the formation of the populous into companies and regiments and the arming of these with many rifles.

> "These all furnished themselves as soon as they could with Arms; form'd themselves into Companies, and Regiments, chose their own Officers, & met every week to be instructed in the manual Exercise, and other Parts of military Discipline. The Women, by subscriptions among themselves, provided silk Colors, which they presented to the Companies, painted with different Devices and Mottos which I supplied".

He was instrumental in the establishment of a hospital and a street sanitation service. All of these accomplishments testify that Franklin was interested in helping the community and its residents as much as he was in furthering his own success. These things have made him a great man in the history of America, someone who will be remembered forever, rather than merely as a successful man who was able to live comfortably.

When writing his Almanack he saw it as a tool for good effect in the community. "I endeavor'd to make it both entertaining and useful ... I therefore filled all the little spaces that occurr'd between the Remarkable Days in the Calendar, with Proverbial Sentences, chiefly such as inculcated Industry and Frugality, as the Means of procuring Wealth and thereby securing Virtue". These proverbs have formed the backbone of today's "*American Wisdom*" and are known by all:

"*A stitch in time saves nine*",
"*A penny saved is a penny earned*",
"*A bird in the hand is worth two in the bush*",
"*An apple a day keeps the doctor away*", and
"*He that goes a borrowing goes a sorrowing*".

All, though not invented by Franklin, were permanently stamped in the American consciousness by his writing.

Many of Franklin's papers were first written for presentation to the Junto. This was an organization of young men devoted to improving the knowledge, skill, and morals of its members. It's existence was kept a secret to prevent "improper persons" from attempting to join, but it was so successful in benefiting its members that they in turn formed their own subordinate organizations to spread the good effect. This may have been the forerunner organizations such as the Elks, Kiwanis, Lions, Rotary, etc.—all with the intention of serving the public and edifying the members.

In 1753 the British sent General Braddock and two Regiments of soldiers to America to fight the French and the Indians. This force had planned to have their weapons and supplies moved through the country on wagons supplied by the colonists of Maryland and Virginia. Unfortunately these people were not able, nor perhaps willing, to provide this support to the British forces. Benjamin Franklin and his son were serving the General at the time and realized that the situation could result in orders to conscript American wagons and drivers by force thus resulting in poor relations and possible bloodshed. To avoid this Franklin volunteered to find wagons and drivers for hire in Pennsylvania. Even with the General's promise of paying good money for their use the people **"insisted on my Bond (Franklin's) for the Performance, which I accordingly gave them."** This put him in the position of being bankrupt should the British not make good on their payments. But it did produce the wagons that were required. For this **"the General too was highly satisfied with my Conduct in procuring him the Wagons, &c. and readily paid my Account of disbursements."** Though there is much more to this incident we see Franklin taking upon himself responsibility for the good of the colonies. These services were not required of him but were volunteered to eliminate a problem that was sure to arise.

Those instances were of civic matters, but he was just as helpful to

Chapter 15: Charity

other men in business matters. As a young man just set up as a printer Franklin found himself short of money and business. At this time a Mr. George House brought in a customer and Franklin states, "**the Gratitude I felt toward House, has made me often more ready, than perhaps I should otherwise have been to assist young Beginners.**" In the course of his life he helped set up several of his apprentices with shops of their own. Thus aiding several families in feeding themselves and providing professions for their sons. Indeed he finally sold his own printing house to another man who ran it successfully.

Later, while experimenting with electricity he saw the opportunity to help another man make a living. "**Mr. Kinnersley, an ingenious Neighbor, who being out of Business, I encouraged to undertake showing the Experiments for money, and drew up for him two Lectures, in which the Experiments were rang'd in such Order and accompanied with Explanations in such Method, as that the foregoing should assist in Comprehending the following.**" Thus a citizen made money with these lectures through Franklin's aid.

Franklin's view of men's conduct in general and public service in particular is that "Those who govern, having much Business on their hands, do not generally like to take the Trouble of considering and carrying into Execution new Projects. The best public Measures are therefore seldom adopted from previous Wisdom, but forc'd by the Occasion."

"Look round the habitable World, how few know their own Good, or knowing it pursue it."

CHARITY:
Search others for their virtues, thyself for thy vices.

LUCKY

FRANKLIN HAD several advantages in his success which he received merely by luck. Before he could get away to New York and Philadelphia he had to escape the indenture to his brother in Boston. As luck would have it, because of some legal problems Benjamin was freed from his indentures but bound by others privately. This left him free to strike out on his own by risking that his brother would not make the private indentures public. Had this situation not occurred he may have remained bound to his brother and never have become the great man he was.

Later, in a letter to his brother-in-law, Robert Omes, he explains why he left Boston and his family. It just so happened that the Governor of the Province, Sir William Keith, was present when the letter arrived and was allowed to read it. Being impressed

A bust of Franklin by Jean-Antoine Houdon.

CHAPTER
16

by the young man, he took the trouble to meet Franklin and later encouraged him to go to London, promising to set him up as a printer. Though this did not work out it did provide Franklin a great amount of experience at a young age.

Franklin also inherited a small legacy when the merchant he worked for died. This was double luck—providing him money and returning him to the printing business, where he was so successful.

Each of these instances can be seen as a break which Franklin had no part in. The freedom from his indentures would have meant nothing had he not been willing to take a risk and strike out for himself. Had he not left home he would never have written a letter and the letter would not have been an impressive one without his appetite for learning. The acquaintance with Governor Keith would have meant little had Franklin been too timid to accept the offer to go to London. And there would have been no inheritance had he not first had the courage to give up printing and to become a merchant's apprentice.

Though each of these events was a lucky break they had no value except that created by Franklin himself. It is the same with all men. Each has built a life and a character through his actions every day. Potentially significant events happen to each and the results depend upon that man's preparation and his response to the events. Those who are prepared and who act boldly will find they encounter opportunity in the same situations where others find calamity. The luck we have is of our own making.

We also find Franklin behaving more generously than he should, trusting his friends to repay him or perhaps unable to refuse to support them. Of his friend Collins, **"He had gam'd too and lost his money, so that I was oblig'd to discharge his Lodgings, & defray his Expenses to and at Philadelphia: which prov'd extremely inconvenient to me."** Later with James Ralph, **"I had 15 Pistoles: So he borrow'd occasionally of me, to subsist while he was looking out for Business."** This money was never repaid. Later he says **"My Friend Ralph had kept me poor. He owed me**

Chapter 16: Lucky

about 27 Pounds; which I was now never likely to receive; a great Sum out of my small Earnings."

This naive behavior extended itself to his relations with Governor Keith. The Governor promised to set him up as a printer and to finance the purchase of equipment in London. This, Franklin believed and traveled to London before learning that there would be no letter of credit and thus no aid in becoming his own master.

LUCKY:
Diligence is the mother of good luck.

HEALTHY

FRANKLIN HAD a very strong ancestry, his father living to be 89, his mother 85, and himself 84. But he also considered health important and attended to it. At age 16, "I happen'd to meet with a Book, written by one Tryon, recommending a Vegetable Diet. I determined to go into it." This diet was inexpensive, leaving more money for books and providing a **"greater Clearness of Head & quicker Apprehension which usually attended Temperance in Eating & Drinking."**

His education through reading also served him well in sickness. "In the Evening I found myself very feverish, & went in to Bed. But having read somewhere that cold water drank plentifully was good for a Fever, I follow'd the Prescription, sweat plentifully most of the Night, my Fever left me, and in the Morning crossing the Ferry, I proceeded on my Journey, on foot, having 50 miles to Bur-

Franklin in 1783, an engraving from a painting by Joseph Duplessis.

CHAPTER 17

ington, where I was told I should find Boats that would carry me the rest of the Way to Philadelphia."

He also understood the weakening effects of beer and the energy provided by good simple food. This he tried to persuade upon others at the printing house in London but had little success.

"At my first Admission into the Printing House, I took to working at Press, imagining I felt a Want of the Bodily Exercise I had been us'd to in America, where Presswork is mix'd with Composing. I drank only Water; the other Workmen, near 50 in Number, were great Guzzlers of Beer. On occasion I carried up & down stairs a large Form of Types in each hand, when others carried but one in both Hands. They wonder'd to see from this & several Instances that the water—American as they call'd me was stronger than themselves who drank strong Beer. We had an Alehouse Boy who attended always in the House to supply the Workmen. My Companion at the Press, drank every day a Pint before Breakfast, a Pint at Breakfast with his Bread and Cheese; a Pint between Breakfast and Dinner; a Pint at Dinner; a Pint in the Afternoon about six o'Clock, and another when he had done his Day's-Work. I thought it a detestable Custom. But it was necessary, he suppos'd, to drink strong Beer that he might be strong to labor. I endeavor'd to convince him that the Bodily Strength afforded by Beer could only be in proportion to the Grain or Flour of the Barley dissolved in the Water of which it was made; that there was more Flour in a Penny-worth of Bread, and therefore if he would eat that with a Pint of Water, it would give him more strength than a Quart of Beer. He drank on however, & had 4 or 5 Shillings to pay out of his Wages every Saturday Night for that muddling Liquor; an Expense I was free from. And thus these poor Devils keep themselves always under."

HEALTHY:

To lengthen thy life, lessen thy meals.

HABITUDES

FRANKLIN'S CONSCIENCE exercised itself upon his life and caused him to turn his attention to the morals he lived by. Like many men he strove unconsciously to live a good life but had no set method for improving is conduct. Then, at the age of 26, he decided to strive for perfection in a methodical manner. "It was about this time that I conceiv'd the bold and arduous Project of arriving at moral Perfection. I wish'd to live without committing any Fault at any time; I would conquer all that either Natural Inclination, Custom, or Company might lead me into. As I knew, or thought I knew, what was right and wrong, I did not see why I might not always do the one and avoid the other."

To attain this perfection he enumerated the primary virtues of life and drew up a book of tables to aid in attaining them. Each table listed the seven days of the week

Memorial marble statue of Benjamin Franklin statue in Philadelphia's Franklin Institute.

CHAPTER
18

across the top and the 13 virtues to be attained down the side. At the top of each page one of the virtues was written. Each day he would judge himself on his faults by placing a red dot next to a virtue that he had offended. But the virtue listed at the top of the page was the primary one to improve that week. With 13 virtues and stressing the perfection of one of these each week he hoped to complete four courses of this study in one year. This attention he hoped would improve his character and eventually take him to perfection. Though the plan did not result in this perfection, even over many years, it did improve his character.

"But on the whole, tho' I never arrived at the Perfection I had been so ambitious to obtain, but fell far short of it, yet I was by the Endeavor a better and a happier Man than I otherwise should have been, if I had not attempted it".

And what were these virtues that this great man was so eager to perfect, the virtues that strengthened him? They are these:

"1. TEMPERANCE.
Eat not to Dullness
Drink not to Elevation.

2. SILENCE.
Speak not but what may benefit others or yourself.
Avoid trifling Conversation.

3. ORDER.
Let all your Things have their Places.
Let each Part of your Business have its Time.

4. RESOLUTION.
Resolve to perform what you ought.
Perform without fail what you resolve.

Chapter 18: Habitudes

5. FRUGALITY.
Make no Expense but to do good to others or yourself: i.e. Waste nothing.

6. INDUSTRY.
Lose no Time. Be always employ'd in something useful. Cut off all unnecessary Actions.

7. SINCERITY.
Use no hurtful Deceit. Think innocently and justly; and, if you speak, speak accordingly.

8. JUSTICE.
Wrong none, by doing Injuries or omitting the Benefits that are your Duty.

9. MODERATION.
Avoid Extremes. Forbear resenting Injuries so much as you think they deserve.

10. CLEANLINESS.
Tolerate no uncleanness in Body, Clothes or Habitation.

11. TRANQUILITY.
Be not disturbed at Trifles, or at Accidents common or unavoidable.

12. CHASTITY.
Rarely use Venery but for Health or Offspring; Never to Dullness, Weakness, or the Injury of your own or another's Peace or Reputation.

13. HUMILITY.
Imitate Jesus and Socrates."

Franklin found this practice and these virtues so valuable that he continued the exercise for some years. And even after ceasing to follow it he always carried the little book with him. Even 57 years after inventing the method Franklin speaks well of its benefits.

"And it may be well my Posterity should be informed, that to this little Artifice, with the Blessing of God, their Ancestor ow'd the constant Felicity of his Life down to his 79th Year in which this is written. What Reverses may attend the Remainder is in the Hand of Providence: But if they arrive the Reflection on past Happiness enjoy'd ought to help his Bearing them with more Resignation. To Temperance he ascribes his long-continu'd Health, & what is still left to him of a good Constitution. To Industry and Frugality the early Easiness of his Circumstances, & Acquisition of his Fortune, with all that knowledge which enabled him to be a useful Citizen, and obtain'd for him some Degree of Reputation among the Learned. To sincerity & Justice the Confidence of his Country, and the honorable Employs it conferr'd upon him. And to the joint Influence of the whole Mass of the Virtues, even in the imperfect State he was able to acquire them, all that Evenness of Temper, & that Cheerfulness in Conversation which makes his Company still sought for, & agreeable even to his younger Acquaintances. I hope therefore that some of my Descendants may follow the Example & reap the Benefit."

THUMBNAIL

TO SUMMARIZE this book in two pages is to enumerate the main characteristics of Benjamin Franklin's life as presented in his Autobiography and to provide an example of each.

Industry and **Frugality** were Franklin's two most cherished and advertized characteristics. These he espouses as being responsible for his wealth and success in business. He recommends them for all who would follow in his steps.

Friendship and valuable acquaintances were never literally credited with responsibility for his success. But in reading the text these stood out as primary in aiding Franklin to his position in the world. He was not a bookish man as we might imagine him. Rather he was a very outgoing and pleasant person, making friends of those about him and often keeping these for a life-time.

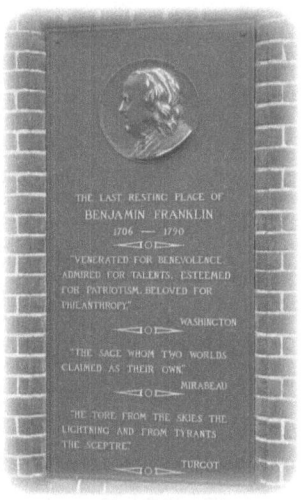

The last resting place of Benjamin Franklin.

CHAPTER
19

Franklin was a voracious **learner**. This he indulged through extensive **reading** and a genuine love of books. His curiosity also lead him often into experimentation such as those with electricity. He was never too old to begin a course of study and was first introduced to electrical phenomena in his 40's.

His primary fame and much of his success was due to his ability to **write**. This he developed through exercises at reproducing the style, substance, and ideas presented in works he admired. His skill made him a success as a printer of pamphlets, newspapers, and almanacs. It also brought him to the attention of the prominent men of Philadelphia and earned him many positions in public service.

He was **independent** and willful as a boy and as man. He had faith in his own opinions and used these to guide his conduct even in the face of opposition from the social mores. These characteristics gave him the confidence to explore, learn and experiment with the unknown.

Franklin believed it best to be **agreeable** with his fellow man and strove to avoid conflict which was not necessary. He believed more could be accomplished through the goodwill of others than through arguing them into your way of thinking. This also expressed itself through his willingness to help others in business and personal matters.

Humility was a characteristic he valued highly, striving to imitate Jesus and Socrates. But he felt that he had not attained humility as much as he had the appearance of it. He was also honest with himself in seeing his faults. These he attributed to himself and did not blame others. This enabled him to work toward alleviating them and thus become a better man.

A man of **good character**, Franklin was bound by what was right. In business this consideration came before that of making money. He was a man who paid his debts, kept his word, and behaved fairly in dealings with others. His success in business was derived from hard work and good, honest relationships with other men. He was wise in conducting his printing house, realizing various opportunities which other's missed

Chapter 19: Thumbnail

and thus coming to dominate the trade in Philadelphia.

Franklin benefitted much from **traveling** about the country. He lived in Boston, New York, Philadelphia, and London. In each place he learned valuable skills and shucked off personal limits placed on him by old acquaintances. This allowed him to grow and advance into higher stations in life with each move. He had a positive outlook on life and refused to be dissuaded by the "croakers" who foresaw only gloom in the future.

He was a **healthy** man due to both heredity and his personal attention to diet and exercise. As a result, he was able to live vigorously to the age of 84. His good habits of reading, writing, and learning lead to many opportunities which could be called luck. But these are more appropriately labeled as being well prepared for the situations that arise in life. He was also generous to friends who were less appreciative and seldom repaid this generosity.

Finally, he strove for moral perfection. Giving attention to becoming a man of **virtue**, he devised various methods for improvement. Though he never reached his ideals he was pleased with the improvement that was gained by the effort.

www.ingramcontent.com/pod-product-compliance
Lightning Source LLC
Chambersburg PA
CBHW031300290426
44109CB00012B/657